# A 24-DAY GUIDED JOURNAL

## FOR SEASONS OF REFLECTION AND TRANSITION

PASSION TALKS
WORKBOOK

ISBN: 9781710928860
Imprint: Independently published
Printed in the United States of America.

Designed by Caleb Durham

passiontalks.org

# TABLE *of* CONTENTS

# ABOUT THIS BOOK

How much do you change in a year? From month to month, we invest in some number of qualities in ourselves and lose touch with other aspects. Do we capitalize on our strengths or work on our weaknesses? Sometimes it's advantageous to pay off an unresolved issue or memory from our past. While other times, it's a better use of our year to move on. This book is designed to guide you through a yearly assessment of your priorities and record a snapshot of what is top of mind for this season.

We hope you enjoy this guided journal. It's intended to be used to reflect, process, dream, and plan. The 24 days are inspired by the Advent days in December, giving room for a fresh start in the new year. Feel free to outline, draw, and sketch, in addition to writing out your thoughts. You can use this book as a point of reflection for next year.

Thanks so much for living out your passions.
*The proceeds of this book help people around the world live out theirs.*

# PRE-ASSESSMENT

Circle a number to rate how strongly you agree or disagree with each of the following statements. Add up the numbers at the end of the assessment.

| STRONGLY DISAGREE | DISAGREE | FEEL NEUTRAL | AGREE | STRONGLY AGREE |
|:---:|:---:|:---:|:---:|:---:|
| 1 | 2 | 3 | 4 | 5 |

1 2 3 4 5     I made good use of this past year

1 2 3 4 5     I understand how my history fits with where I am going

1 2 3 4 5     I have a good sense of where I want to be in the future

1 2 3 4 5     I can clearly identify my passions

1 2 3 4 5     I have a strong sense of my mission and purpose

1 2 3 4 5     I have clear role models and idea of the type of person I want to be

1 2 3 4 5     I am able to forgive others and myself for past transgressions

1 2 3 4 5     I understand why the past year turned out the way it did

1 2 3 4 5     It is clear where I am growing and where I need to grow

1 2 3 4 5     I have a clear sense of my priorities

1 2 3 4 5     I do not have non-constructive negative thoughts about myself

1 2 3 4 5         I have confidence in the movements, groups, and people with whom I affiliate

1 2 3 4 5         I have a clear vision for the sort of world I would like see

1 2 3 4 5         If someone offered me resources or help, I would know how to use it

1 2 3 4 5         I am aware of what needs to change in my life

1 2 3 4 5         I have a firm understanding of my belief system

1 2 3 4 5         I can identify and describe the impact of my projects in the past year

1 2 3 4 5         I can explain the relevance of my past accomplishments

1 2 3 4 5         I can articulate the value of my experiences

1 2 3 4 5         I can confidently outline the credibility of my beliefs and goals

1 2 3 4 5         I have a sense of initiative and plan for reaching my mission and goals

1 2 3 4 5         I have the ambition and drive to accomplish my mission and goals

1 2 3 4 5         I have a clear idea of what I will and will not do next year

1 2 3 4 5         It is not hard to be grateful for what I have

Total Count:        Today's Date:

# PRESENT

---

We're going to get started by giving this calendar year a title. What would you call it?

_____
(Your Year's Title)

Now, let's look back month by month at your recent accomplishments.
What are some things you've done in the past year? Projects you've finished? Goals you've met?
What did you discover or experience? _In this month's box, write what are you currently working on._

| January | February |
|---|---|
|  |  |
| March | April |
|  |  |

| May | June |
|---|---|
| July | August |
| September | October |
| November | December |

# PAST

———

What's your origin story? Think about where you came from, moments that defined you, decisions that changed your trajectory, etc. When someone asks you about your back-story, what do you tell them?

_____

(Autobiography Title)

## WRITE ABOUT ONE OF YOUR FIRST MEMORIES.
## DOES IT TELL YOU ANYTHING ABOUT WHO YOU ARE TODAY?

SUMMARIZE WHAT YOU KNOW ABOUT YOU PARENTS AND GIVE CONTEXT TO THE CIRCUMSTANCES FOR WHICH YOU WERE BORN.

IF YOU COULD BREAK DOWN THE YEARS OF YOUR LIFE INTO CHAPTERS, WHAT WOULD THEY BE?

14

# FUTURE

———

Looking forward over the life we hope to live helps focus and shape the decisions we make in the present. Where do you see yourself in the future? What will you accomplish? What is the sort of world you would like to see?

## NEXT YEAR

**5 YEARS FROM NOW**

**10 YEARS FROM NOW**

# PASSIONS

---

What are you most passionate about? What are the things you spend the most time doing? What do you find yourself enjoying the most? Starting at the top of the following page, write your #1 priority, and then list the two runner ups, and continue to rank your passions all the way down. *Feel free to use this page to brainstorm.*

# MISSION

---

Sometimes it can be hard to know how to move forward without a clear sense of purpose. Synthesizing your passions into a short, working mission statement can be a really helpful way to prioritize goals and make sure you're following through with them. In this chapter of your life, what is your mission statement?

**CAUSE** WRITE DOWN A PEOPLE GROUP, COLLECTIVE, OR CAUSE DO YOU CONNECT WITH MOST.

**IDEALS** CIRCLE UP TO 3 OBJECTIVES THAT RESONATE WITH YOU.

| | | | | | | |
|---|---|---|---|---|---|---|
| Charity | Kindness | Faith | Safety | Hope | Truth | Justice |
| Excellence | Respect | Honor | Trust | Joy | Equality | Relationships |
| Honesty | Simplicity | Integrity | Dignity | Positivity | Freedom | Service |
| Inner Peace | Commitment | Love | Family | Self-worth | Humility | Wholeness |

## **ACTIONS** CIRCLE UP TO 3 VERBS THAT RESONATE WITH YOU.

| | | | | | | |
|---|---|---|---|---|---|---|
| Accomplish | Summon | Relate | Possess | Light | Foster | Dream |
| Compel | Advance | Sustain | Remember | Prepare | Master | Generate |
| Encourage | Compose | Alleviate | Translate | Respect | Progress | Mediate |
| Identify | Enlighten | Consider | Believe | Utilize | Revise | Provide |
| Motivate | Improve | Entertain | Council | Build | Venture | Save |
| Reduce | Organize | Integrate | Expand | Direct | Claim | Work |
| Share | Reform | Perform | Launch | Facilitate | Distribute | Command |
| Acquire | Support | Relax | Practice | Make | Franchise | Educate |
| Compete | Affect | Take | Renew | Present | Mature | Give |
| Engage | Confirm | Amplify | Understand | Restore | Promise | Model |
| Illuminate | Enlist | Construct | Bestow | Validate | Safeguard | Realize |
| Negotiate | Improvise | Evaluate | Create | Cause | Verbalize | Sell |
| Refine | Overcome | Involve | Explore | Discover | Collect | Write |
| Speak | Regard | Play | Lead | Forgive | Draft | Communicate |
| Adopt | Surrender | Release | Praise | Manifest | Further | Embrace |
| Compliment | Affirm | Trade | Resonate | Produce | Measure | Grant |
| Enhance | Connect | Ascend | Use | Return | Promote | Mold |
| Implement | Enliven | Continue | Brighten | Value | Satisfy | Reclaim |
| Nurture | Inspire | Excite | Demonstrate | Choose | Volunteer | Serve |
| Reflect | Participate | Know | Extend | Discuss | Combine | Yield |

## **MISSION STATEMENT**

"CURRENTLY, I HOPE TO _____ _____
(actions)                                                                    (ideals)
(TO/FOR/WITH/THROUGH) _____ ."
                                          (cause)

*Adapted from "The Path: Creating Your Mission Statement for Work and for Life"*

# INSPIRATION

Today, think about the people who inspire and amaze you. Who do you respect and admire? Who do you wish you were more like? Write down their names, and how they inspire you. Make a point to tell them sometime soon, if they are still in your life.

**WHO DO I ADMIRE MOST?**

WHO CAN I GO TO FOR WISE COUNSEL?

WHO SHOULD I SPEND MORE TIME GETTING TO KNOW?

# FORGIVENESS

—————

Are there interactions, mistakes, misunderstandings, and mistakes that carry shame, guilt, and regret? As you seek forgiveness, forgive yourself and others, you can shed all of those misgivings.

## WHO ARE 3 PEOPLE I SHOULD FORGIVE?

WHO ARE 3 PEOPLE FROM WHOM I SHOULD SEEK FORGIVENESS?

WHAT ARE 3 AREAS/MEMORIES FOR WHICH I SHOULD FORGIVE MYSELF?

# UNDERSTANDING

———

Your experiences shape the understanding of your life. A lot can change in a year, so take time to recognize the fruits of your efforts. Record and reflect on the greatest lessons you learned this year, and make the most of your efforts by reflecting on them.

## WHAT DID I LEARN AND GROW THE MOST FROM IN THIS PAST YEAR?

HOW COULD I HAVE DONE BETTER?

WHAT WERE THE MOST DIFFICULT THINGS I DID LAST YEAR?

WHAT WERE THE MOST REWARDING THINGS I DID LAST YEAR?

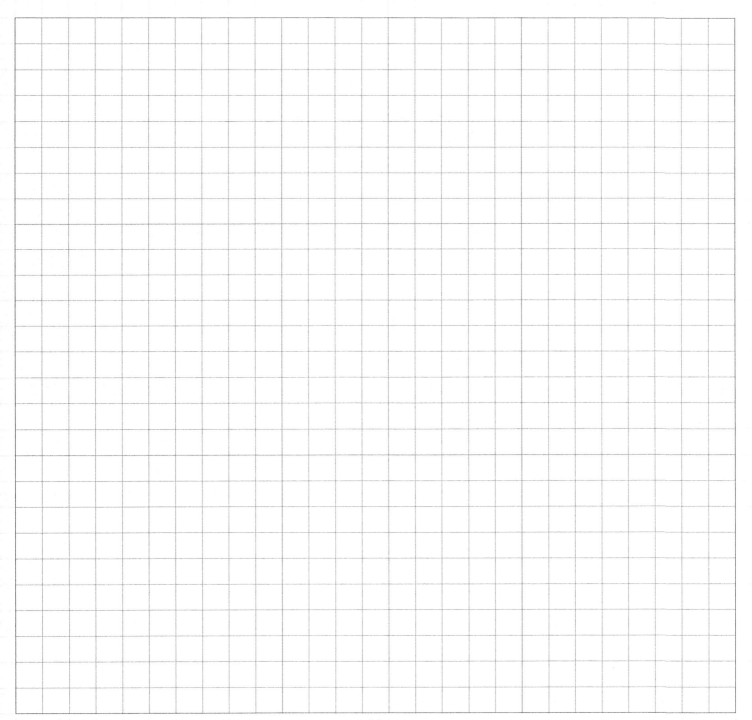

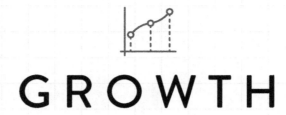

# GROWTH

———

Do you desire to be more disciplined, healthier, more patient, kind or compassionate? Write about your opportunities for growth, starting with general areas of focus; then outline specific tasks that you are setting for yourself.

**WHICH AREAS DO I WANT TO FOCUS ON DEVELOPING IN MY OWN LIFE?**

# RANK THE THINGS YOU NEED TO DO FROM MOST TO LEAST CHALLENGING. CIRCLE THE OPPORTUNITIES THAT EXCITE YOU MOST.

1

2

3

4

5

6

7

8

9

10

# BUCKET YOUR TO-DO LIST BY WRITING EACH NUMBER IN THE BOXES:

|  | Urgent | Not Urgent |
|---|---|---|
| Important |  |  |
| Not Important |  |  |

# PRIORITIES

---

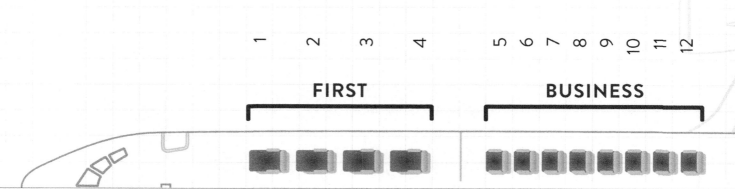

FIRST | BUSINESS

Imagine you only have a few seats for first-class and business-class, while the most seats are in economy. Fill the seats with your priorities. Feel free to leave empty seats to make space for emergent needs.

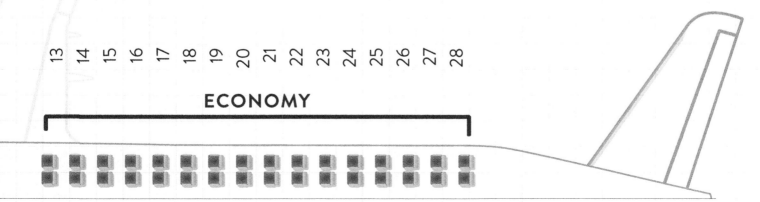

13 14 15 16 17 18 19 20 21 22 23 24 25 26 27 28

**ECONOMY**

# IDENTITY

———

Today we are going to take a close look at our inner-self and the things we believe.
As you identify the lies that you believe about yourself and exchange them for the truth, you will be able to access breakthrough.

## WHAT ARE YOUR FEARS?

## WHAT ARE YOUR BEST QUALITIES?

WHAT ARE THE LIES YOU BELIEVE ABOUT YOURSELF?

WHAT IS THE TRUTH THAT OPPOSES EACH OF THOSE LIES?

WHAT WOULD CHANGE IN YOUR LIFE IF YOU BELIEVED THOSE TRUTHS?

# PARTNERSHIP

———

Which organizations/groups/movements/people do you want to partner with in this season? Countless opportunities are looking for help; which relationships are you going to focus on? Which organizations or people have a mission that you believe in, credibility in that space, and are a good fit for collaboration?

| Organization Name | Mission/Purpose of Organization | People/Points of Contact There |
|---|---|---|
| | | |

| Organization Name | Mission/Purpose of Organization | People/Points of Contact There |
|---|---|---|
| | | |

# VISION

---

What does a better world look like? Even if we can't solve everything at once, we can still hold to the vision of what a better world would be. As we grow our faith in that better world, our hope also increases.

## WHAT ARE THE BIGGEST PROBLEMS FACING YOUR...

world?

community?

society?

family?

# HOW WOULD YOU LIKE TO IMPROVE THOSE SITUATIONS?

# WHAT SHOULD THINGS BE LIKE IN YOUR...

world?

community?

society?

family?

# RESOURCES

———

Itemize a mock fundraising proposal. People are more likely to contribute resources toward a specific ask. It helps to have an idea for how to distribute, utilize, and grow such provision as you plan. You never know when an opportunity will present itself.

## WHAT WOULD YOU DO IF SOMEONE GAVE YOU...

$100 USD?

$1,000 USD?

$10,000 USD?

$100,000 USD?

$1,000,000 USD?

$1,000,000,000 USD?

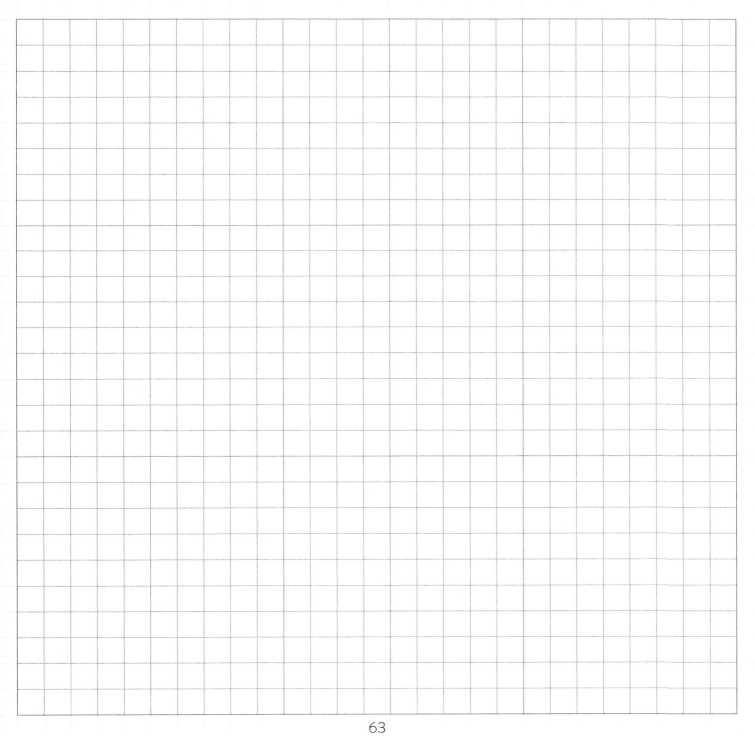

# RESOLUTION

———

This is a retrospective on your past year and how to clear out the old in order to make space for the new. What got you to where you are today isn't necessarily what will help you get to where you need to be tomorrow. What do you want to change about yourself for the next year?

## WHAT ARE THINGS THAT I WILL STOP DOING IN THE NEXT YEAR?

## WHAT ARE THINGS THAT I WILL START DOING IN THE NEXT YEAR?

## WHAT ARE THINGS THAT I WILL CONTINUE DOING IN THE NEXT YEAR?

# BELIEF

---

Write or outline a statement of your beliefs. Why do you do what you do in life? What motivates you?

WHAT LABELS, GROUPS, CREEDS, PHILOSOPHIES, OR RELIGIONS DO YOU LIVE BY OR BORROW FROM? DESCRIBE HOW AND WHAT YOU'VE INCORPORATED INTO YOUR LIFE.

WHEN HAVE YOU HAD MAJOR CHANGES TO YOUR FAITH OR BELIEFS? DESCRIBE YOUR EPIPHANIES AND SPIRITUAL EXPERIENCES.

LIST SPIRITUAL OR MINDFULNESS PRACTICES THAT HELP YOU OR THAT YOU ARE MOST DRAWN TO.

Passion  Talk #1

# PROJECT

_____

If you were to give a talk about a project you've completed, which project would you pick?

What is the abstract/summary of your talk?

_____

(Talk Title)

Professional 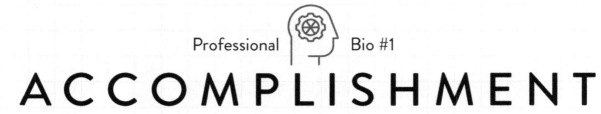 Bio #1

# ACCOMPLISHMENT

---

Write or outline a bio for yourself. Introduce yourself and who you are. Why should people listen to you tell the story about the project you are describing on Day 17?

Passion Talk #2

# EXPERIENCE

---

If you were to give a talk about something you know a lot about, what would it be? What is the abstract/summary of your talk?

_____

(Talk Title)

DAY 19

Professional Bio #2

# CREDIBILITY

———

Write a bio for yourself. Introduce yourself and who you are. Why should people listen to you talk about the concepts described on Day 19? What gives your credibility? We all have the ability to speak into things, but why would someone listen to you speak?

Day 21

Passion         Talk #3

# INITIATIVE

---

If you were to give a talk about something you would like to see happen or are working towards, what would it be? What is the abstract/summary of your talk?

_____

(Talk Title)

Professional Bio #3

# AMBITION

———

Write or outline a bio for yourself. Introduce yourself and who you are. Why should people listen to you describe the initiative you outlined on Day 21?

DAY 22

# PLANNING

---

Just like we did on Day 1, when we reflected on recent accomplishments, we also want to draw out a roadmap for the upcoming months. Plan out your next year by sketching out your commitments, hopes, and plans.

| January | February |
|---|---|
|  |  |
| March | April |
|  |  |

| May | June |
|---|---|
| July | August |
| September | October |
| November | December |

# GRATITUDE

---

For our final exercise, we are coming back around to the place of thankfulness.

## WHAT ARE YOU THANKFUL FOR?

WHO SHOULD YOU THANK?

WRITE A TO-DO LIST OF THINGS YOU FEEL INSPIRED TO DO
BEFORE THE END OF THE YEAR:

# POST-ASSESSMENT

Circle a number to rate how strongly you agree or disagree with each of the following statements. Add up the numbers at the end of the assessment.

| STRONGLY DISAGREE | DISAGREE | FEEL NEUTRAL | AGREE | STRONGLY AGREE |
|:---:|:---:|:---:|:---:|:---:|
| 1 | 2 | 3 | 4 | 5 |

1 2 3 4 5    I made good use of this past year

1 2 3 4 5    I understand how my history fits with where I am going

1 2 3 4 5    I have a good sense of where I want to be in the future

1 2 3 4 5    I can clearly identify my passions

1 2 3 4 5    I have a strong sense of my mission and purpose

1 2 3 4 5    I have clear role models and idea of the type of person I want to be

1 2 3 4 5    I am able to forgive others and myself for past transgressions

1 2 3 4 5    I understand why the past year turned out the way it did

1 2 3 4 5    It is clear where I am growing and where I need to grow

1 2 3 4 5    I have a clear sense of my priorities

1 2 3 4 5    I do not have non-constructive negative thoughts about myself

**1 2 3 4 5**         I have confidence in the movements, groups, and people with whom I affiliate

**1 2 3 4 5**         I have a clear vision for the sort of world I would like see

**1 2 3 4 5**         If someone offered me resources or help, I would know how to use it

**1 2 3 4 5**         I am aware of what needs to change in my life

**1 2 3 4 5**         I have a firm understanding of my belief system

**1 2 3 4 5**         I can identify and describe the impact of my projects in the past year

**1 2 3 4 5**         I can explain the relevance of my past accomplishments

**1 2 3 4 5**         I can articulate the value of my experiences

**1 2 3 4 5**         I can confidently outline the credibility of my beliefs and goals

**1 2 3 4 5**         I have a sense of initiative and plan for reaching my mission and goals

**1 2 3 4 5**         I have the ambition and drive to accomplish my mission and goals

**1 2 3 4 5**         I have a clear idea of what I will and will not do next year

**1 2 3 4 5**         It is not hard to be grateful for what I have

| Total Count: | Today's Date: |
| --- | --- |

# FINAL THOUGHTS

As you've gone through this book, you have intentionally connected with your passions, dreams, and priorities. You've cleared distractions like unforgiveness and lies out of your way, and you've practiced, planned, and workshopped for the future. You've also written out summaries for three talks, blog posts, or videos that are meaningful to you.

As you continue to develop your passions, we hope that this journal becomes an annual practice. As you change from season to season, chapter to chapter, we welcome you to revisit and continue to reflect on your journey.

Thanks for supporting others on their journey as well.

*To stay in touch or give feedback, please visit*
**WWW.PASSIONWORKBOOK.COM**

Made in the USA
Middletown, DE
05 February 2021

33018527R00064